THE RIGHT SHOES

A JOURNEY OF SELF-DISCOVERY AND MEANINGFUL CONNECTIONS

Le grá
Lucy

ORLA KELLY
PUBLISHING

LUCY CRONLY

978-1-915502-78-0

All rights reserved. ©2025 Lucy Cronly

All intellectual property rights including copyright, design right and publishing rights rest with the author. No part of this book may be reproduced or transmitted in any way including any written, electronic, recording, or photocopying without written permission of the author. This publication is intended for information purpose and is based on the author›s knowledge and experience working in the sector. Published in Ireland by Orla Kelly Publishing.

Orla Kelly Publishing
27 Kilbrody,
Mount Oval,
Rochestown,
Cork,
Ireland.

Testimonials

I'm delighted to recommend Lucy Cronly Coaching, to my friends and family.

During a one-to-one session we had over the Summer, Lucy spotted a blind spot I didn't even know I had. Her approach is refreshingly supportive, nudging me to step out of my comfort zone while keeping things light-hearted.

Lucy's guidance has already given me practical steps to build real momentum in my professional life.

If you're not aiming to be 'better than the rest' but to be the best version of yourself, and maybe have a laugh along the way Lucy's the coach to get you there! - **Benny Sheridan**

I entered into coaching with Lucy to find the drive and confidence needed to start a new venture in my life. I am coming out of burnout and the 'worry monster' inside me was having a field day.

My sessions with Lucy gave me a neutral space to work out what was blocking me from starting this new phase in my life. Through the coaching, I managed to focus on the passion and driving force needed to move forward and silence the self-limiting thoughts.

Lucy is a fantastic coach who I would highly recommend. I wish Lucy all the best with her future endeavours. - **Claudia**

Lucy Cronly is a superb Coach. I have been coached by her for various issues in my life and in all sessions with me, she proved herself to be level-headed, calm, reassuring in her presence, totally there for me and in every regard full of heart for me as the client and the process we were working through.

Lucy has vast experience and expertise and is a total 'People Person', which is a lovely trait combined with integrity and pristine professionalism. I did my research and actually met with a number of coaches before I chose Lucy. Plus she has vast life experience herself, so she really understood me. By the way, she misses nothing! In other words, Lucy is a great listener, but with that said, she respectfully challenges and probes to get to the bottom of things. I could go on, but suffice to say Lucy is a master in her coaching practice and I would highly recommend her to assist you in achieving your potential. - **Colette Doris**

Definitely take this program, it will be incredibly worthwhile and you won't regret it. The biggest takeaway from this is that you are the only version of yourself that exists and therefore have the right to live because you were born into this world. Thank you so much Lucy. Thanks for all the guidance I'm so glad I went. - **Adolescent 17**

Lucy was my first manager in my social care career and set the bar on management and leadership very high. Lucy's ability to lead and manage a team while also ensuring individual team members excel in their own skill set has always stayed with me throughout my career. Lucy is skilled in supporting individuals to reflect and assess their own practice, focussing on the positives and correcting underperformance. In team situations, she has the ability to ensure all voices are heard while leading the team to collective decisions for the betterment of the service or individuals they are supporting.

In project management, Lucy breaks down the task to achievable steps, assigning work to those people best placed to achieve the desired results within their skill set. Her ability to know her teams' strengths and weaknesses assists her in this task, ensuring that the end goal is always achieved.

Lucy's loyalty, honesty, and integrity are the most important traits that I have taken from my experience working with her, into my own career. The loyalty to provide the very best care and to support the service users, the honesty to tell the truth and reality of the situation, and to respect people's ability to manage this honestly and the integrity and willingness to do things right.

Lucy's skill set as a manager has greatly influenced my own management style and her abilities as a manager is something I aspire too. - **Lorraine Costello, Early Years Inspector**

I would tell anyone to work with Lucy. They could get some vital skills for their future. My biggest takeaway was learning about myself. I found the (work) sheets useful and I may look back on them when in trouble. Wisdom is a wonderful thing! - **Adolescent 15**

Lucy is a professional coach with powerful and structured coaching techniques. At the end of being coached by Lucy, I realised for the first time in my life that the wild curiosity which had always driven me to distraction was actually a unique and powerful superpower that has always opened doors for me and allowed me to transform the lives of my own coaching clients. I really recommend Lucy as a coach, especially for families and young people that want to understand themselves and the world around them better. - **Ryan**

I say do Lucy's coaching program because you learn something you didn't know existed. My biggest takeaway was about how many different types of listening there are. - **Adolescent 16**

I really enjoyed working together and listening to everyone's stories/ knowledge. It was a wonderful experience and I have learned a lot. The course was very informative and I took so much away with me each week. Habits/choices and being full of myself and no one else. I loved the winning video and changing our thoughts to believe we are winning every day. Lucy you're a superstar, thanks so much. - **Adult course participant**

Very positive, welcoming, nurturing secure safe environment. Everybody appeared to feel included, heard and valued. Thank you, Lucy, I really enjoyed this course. - **Adult course participant**

For me, she is full of herself, well who else would she be full of really resonated with me. I plan to implement the tools on a daily basis and trust and believe in myself. - **Adult course participant**

Dedicated to Nigel, Liam, Eoin and Niall.

Acknowledgements

Innovation rests on the shoulders of giants, with each of us building on the knowledge and wisdom that came before. This book is my contribution to that ongoing legacy – a gesture of gratitude to the vast array of thinkers who have paved the way.

My journey into Coaching With Neuroscience began with the Positive Success Group, which allowed me to expand my thinking and explore self-awareness. Through their Full Personal Review, I was able to evaluate my impact on the world and make purposeful choices about my path forward. My heartfelt thanks go to Maureen Hewitt, master coach and academic director, for her wisdom and guidance throughout the process.

To my friends, colleagues, and fellow coaches, thank you for your encouragement and belief in my work. A special thanks to Colette Doris, life coach and yoga teacher, who helped me navigate challenging moments with grace.

To my tutors and fellow students at UCD Innovation Academy, thank you for nurturing my idea, helping it to flourish, and encouraging me to keep moving forward. Your stories and insights enriched this work and provided the foundation for growth.

To my Trim Shed ladies, thank you for the encouragement and support, especially Cindy, who will get the first signed copy of this book!

A warm thanks to my BNI network, the 'I know a guy' group, especially Liliane Scully and Lane Farber, whose connections led me to the talented Orla Kelly. Orla, it has been an incredible experience working with you – your guidance, straightforwardness, and vision have been invaluable. Thanks to Louise McSharry for creating a beautiful cover and designs that brought this book to life.

To everyone who shared their stories about shoes, thank you for the connections, reflections, and your time. And a very special thanks to my Uncle Eddie for sharing memories of my mother's family, bringing me back to the warmth of my grandparents. My mother passed away fifty years ago this Monday, November 4, 2024, and I hope this book is something she would have appreciated and enjoyed.

To my sister, Susan, thank you for your unwavering support, belief in me, and invaluable insights.

Finally, to my family – my husband, Nigel, for supporting me through bold and sometimes mad ideas, and my three sons, Liam, Eoin, and Niall, who keep me grounded and constantly growing. You are my heart.

Contents

Testimonials iii
Dedicated vii
Acknowledgements ix
How This Book Came About 1
Who Should Read This Book? 4
My Promise to You 5
About the Author 6
My Gift to You 8
Introduction 10
Shoes That Bring Joy 13
Admiring Someone's Shoes 15
Shoes That Explore Difficult Things 18
Stories of Others 21
One Of Those Days 25
Wrong Shoes/Right Place – Right Shoes/Wrong Place 28
Powering Up! 30
Bare Feet 34

Walk in My Shoes for a Day: The Power of Empathy 38
Auditing Our Shoe Collection 40
Owning Your Own Footsteps 42
Self-Audit 44
Gathering the Wisdom: Shoe Stories 56
Next Steps 74
Reflection 81
Work With Lucy 84
Bonus Item: A History of Shoes and Fun Facts 86
Please Review 90
Appendix 1 91
References 93

How This Book Came About

The idea for this book began in November 2023 on the last day of a study module on creativity at University College Dublin. I was pursuing a Level 9 Professional Diploma in Creativity, Innovation and Leadership, and the task was to reflect on the week of work completed and consider the topic for our end-of-year project. We were to spend some time alone with our thoughts outside by the lake. I walked along the grass, which was slippery in places, and then onto the tarmac, which allowed for more grip and felt safer. My footsteps were almost silent, reminding me of when my son was sick in hospital with cancer. He was eleven at diagnosis. I always wore silent shoes in Crumlin Hospital, as they helped me feel less visible and less present. I know now it was a coping mechanism, one I later realised I had used many times in my life.

As I walked along reflecting on this time, I found gravel, and there was a groundedness about crunching around on the crushed stone, a strong sense of presence and connectedness to the space I was in. Watching my feet walk through the different spaces, I was struck by the correlation between shoes and how we show up in the world. I realised that if I were to complete the task I was given, I would have to put on a pair of noisy shoes, show up, and get my paper and presentation done. Standing up in front of a group to make a presentation alone would require a pair of noisy shoes!

Usually, when I'm out walking, I take in the world around me or step into reflective mode, going within. However, on this particular walk, my attention shifted downward to my shoes. Instantly, I was reminded of the joyful shopping spree with my sister, Susan, when I bought them. These shoes weren't just footwear; they were a symbol of joy and connection from that delightful evening. They carried stories of kindness and support. I had purchased the shoes using vouchers given to me by a PhD student to say thank you for helping her, and I was able to get a 10 percent discount on the shoes using my UCD student card, one of the wonderful perks of being a student. The shoes didn't cost me any money, as the voucher and discount covered the cost. This started a curiosity. In the weeks following that day in UCD, I noticed shoes more and more, so I started asking questions about people's shoes, starting with people I knew well along with admiring the shoes of strangers. It opened a treasure trove of stories, a glimpse into the narratives we have about ourselves, a glimpse of dreams, a glimpse of values. People I didn't know and had never met before shared very personal stories about themselves simply from me admiring their shoes.

I asked myself, *Could the story of our shoes create an accessible space for narrative and exploration?*

'I only ever buy the same shoes', my husband Nigel said – this got me thinking about acknowledging the power of small steps and subtle change.

He didn't think his shoes told any story because he had bought the same style of shoes for over twenty years. We reflected on this before he realised that each pair of shoes he bought was as close as possible to the previous pair, but there was a very marked difference between the first pair he'd bought and the current pair. This example can be viewed as a metaphor for how we think we are staying the same, but tiny, incremental changes over time can go unnoticed and lead to bigger changes than we realise.

I presented my 'the right shoes' idea to a group, and a story was shared afterwards. 'An old girlfriend of mine used to say you could tell a lot about a person from their shoes. She then dumped me; I guess I didn't have the right shoes!' (Michael S.).

Who Should Read This Book?

I wrote this book for *you* – if you're ready to take control of your narrative and share your story with authenticity. Imagine stepping forward each day with purpose, excitement, and a heart full of possibilities. Let this book serve as your guide.

Feeling overwhelmed or unsure of where to start? Think you're too busy to find those essential moments of calm? *Think again*. You will be shown how to effortlessly weave reflective practices into your daily routine.

Want to be more present in your life? Curious about how your actions impact those around you? You will be provided with tools for self-awareness, allowing you to truly connect with yourself and others on a deeper level.

You see, this is more than just a book; it's an opportunity – to reflect on who you are, explore what you're seeking, and plant the seeds for becoming the very best version of yourself.

Living your life to be the best version of yourself rather than being better than the rest reaches for growth, learning, finding joy and happiness, and ultimately being your authentic self, living to your values and getting out of your own way.

My Promise to You

I promise to guide you on a fun, accessible, and meaningful journey toward deepening your connections – with yourself and with others. Along the way, we'll plant seeds of insight to help you cultivate a life of greater happiness. Why aim for 'happier' and not just 'happy'? Because happiness is a lifelong journey, a constantly evolving experience without a final destination. In every moment there is something you can do to be happier, regardless of the starting point.

But before we begin, let me share a little about myself.

About the Author

My name is Lucy Cronly, and I live in Trim with my husband, Nigel, and three sons, Liam, Eoin, and Niall. An unending curiosity about people, life, and learning drives me professionally and personally. I thrive on connecting with others, listening to their unique stories, and understanding their challenges, joys, loves, and wisdom.

I am a compassionate and energetic professional coach with a focus on neuroscience. My approach to coaching is holistic, involving heart, head, and gut to help clients form meaningful connections with themselves and others. I firmly believe that even the most complex theories about human interaction can be simplified and understood by everyone.

My coaching philosophy centres on the belief that every individual is creative, resourceful, and whole. I believe that everyone should be their own best friend, and I coach with this in mind. That way you will always have someone with you who is kind and empathetic and holds you accountable. With these principles at the forefront, I support and guide clients in uncovering their true desires and implementing strategic actions to achieve their goals. I empower them to understand themselves better, make informed choices, and move forward confidently.

I am highly organised and detail oriented, bridging the gap between individuals and their potential, enabling them to realise their vision for themselves. Through empathy, kindness, creativity, and challenging coaching conversations, I help clients embrace the way forward and achieve success with personalised support, guidance, and expertise.

*Let me hold
the door for you
I may have
never walked
in your shoes
but I can see
your soles are worn
your strength is torn
under the weight of a story
I have never lived before
Let me hold the door for you
After all you have walked through
It is the least I can do
—Morgan Harper Nichols*

My Gift to You

This book will plant seeds for transformational thinking that will allow you to live a happier life. The idea is that by choosing your shoes, you create meaning, living in the moment and planning for where you want to go. Being curious about other people's shoes can create opportunities to build meaningful connections and provide insight into how they see the world.

Using the playful theme of shoes and conversations about them, you will be shown how to become your own best friend.

With a touch of humour and fun, this book guides you toward smart thinking about your desires and how to align yourself to achieve them. Using shoes as a visual to create a pause – a space for thought, awareness, and paying attention to what serves you best – discover how to tap into the power and patience of ordinary things.

The Patience of Ordinary Things

It is a kind of love, is it not?
How the cup holds the tea,
How the chair stands sturdy and foursquare,
How the floor receives the bottoms of shoes
Or toes. How soles of feet know
Where they're supposed to be.
I've been thinking about the patience
Of ordinary things, how clothes
Wait respectfully in closets
And soap dries quietly in the dish,
And towels drink the wet
From skin of the back.
And the lovely repetition of stairs.
And what is more generous than a window?

—Pat Schneider

Used by permission of the estate of Pat Schneider

Introduction

My intention with this book is to create a pathway for you to build meaningful threads of connection with yourself and others. Let's delve into the story behind your shoes, reflecting on whether you chose them intentionally or not. Consider the meaningful narratives we can create about our present and future by examining what we wear on our feet, what we aspire to wear, and how these choices accompany us on our life journey. This aligns with my purpose: to listen with heart, head, and gut so we can build meaningful connections with ourselves and others. Stopping to create intention in our day by choosing our shoes can set us up nicely for the day ahead.

Reflecting on shoes can also provide an intimate glimpse into the thinking and values of another person in an easy manner. Telling someone you love their shoes can elicit a story, creating connection and intimacy without intrusion or crossing boundaries.

Talking about shoes can give us insight into ourselves and others in a nonintrusive way. The medium of shoes can provide a means of "externalising the problem" and prompt meaningful conversation about ourselves. Seeing the conversation as somewhat separate from the person can create space for exploration.

Could using the shoe metaphor create opportunities to bring meaning to our lives, better understand our narratives, and make more conscious choices that serve us well? Yes it can! Let me show you how.

> *You have brains in your head*
> *You have feet in in your shoes*
> *You can steer yourself in any direction you choose*
> *You're on your own and you know what you know*
> *And you are the one who'll decide where to go*
> **—Dr Seuss**

Sharing the idea of shoes as a segue into conversation with others has made me aware of the many sayings we have about shoes – a simple shorthand that tells a bigger story.

A pebble in my shoe . . .

Walk in my shoes for a day . . .

The next best step . . .

Every journey begins with the first step . . .

Each expression tells a story of how we move through the world, encounter obstacles, seek to understand each other, and strive forward.

What pain point could the exploration of shoes address? It could be a way to gather people, share stories, hear the stories of others, and think about being purposeful in a fun and relatable way. I have taken many photos of shoes over the years; they each tell a story. Exploring our narratives through our shoes could allow us to understand ourselves better and be mindful of how we step into different situations.

Could exploration of our shoes offer a fun route into self-exploration in a manner that has depth and meaning, provides glimmers of self-understanding, and is purposeful and intentional, rather than triggering self-doubt that can hold us back from being our best self?

Let's explore this further with some photographs I have been gathering. I didn't realise I had so many photos of shoes until I looked through my phone. I even have a short video I made on New Year's Eve, throwing my old slippers in the bin at midnight and putting on a new pair of my favourite slippers. You will find it on my website if you are up for a giggle!

Shoes That Bring Joy

Stopping to consider how shoes bring joy made me think of my slippers. This photo of my slippers in front of the fire, where I am tucked up with a knitting project, brings me joy. I love my cosy slippers, worn at home, my happiest place. When I step in from a busy day to relax among familiar voices, I kick off the outside world and pop on my slippers. Sometimes it is enough just knowing this is how the day will end and that my slippers are waiting by the door.

The fabulous pink shoes in this photo were dyed in anticipation of a day out to watch the movie premieres of *Barbie* and *Oppenheimer* (also known as Barbenheimer). We booked and paid for our tickets weeks in advance. There was excitement and lots of conversations in preparation for the event; we were on a mission to set up something fun. I spent the day with one of my sons as we enjoyed the two movies, ate together, and talked easily in each other's company—a time of connection and sharing.

The third pair are pink with red hearts in my favourite material – suede pure joy! Just to add to the pleasure, I got them on sale!

Having shoes that convey happy memories can uplift our spirits on tough days, when we need something extra to support us. Carrying these positive memories can help us access courage and strength when we are facing something difficult, or it can simply add an extra smile to the day.

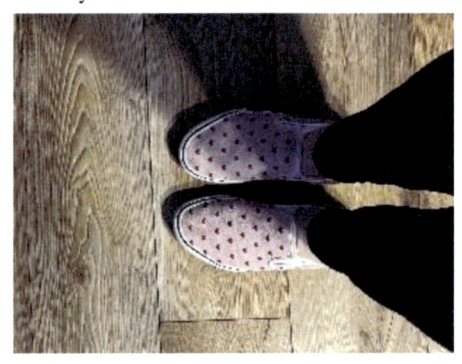

Admiring Someone's Shoes

I said your hair looked amazing but what I really wanted to say was 'Your energy sparks a little bit of something in mine, your smile warms my heart, and when you laugh, I just have to laugh too, it's like a bubbling stream of fresh water running through my soul. I feel like the sun is shining on me when you're near and when I leave you, sad as it is, I feel like I've been charged, plugged into the mains for an infusion of fizz and life.' But I said 'I love your shoes' instead. I hope you heard what I really meant.
—Donna Ashworth

Saying 'I love your shoes' to another person can open a story about where the shoes came from and what intention they brought. It can be a simple way of connecting with another person, a way of appreciating or admiring them with a few words when you can't find the right ones.

I wonder who was the first person to wear runners rather than high heels with a dress? Who was the second person to think it was a great idea? Look how the trend grew and was embraced. Did someone say 'I love your shoes', and in that moment, seeds of ideas and connection were planted to grow a new and way-more-comfortable trend?

Saying 'I love your shoes' can open the door to stories about where the shoes came from and the intentions they carry. It's a simple way of connecting with someone, offering admiration when words might otherwise fall short. Like a silent poem, it says, *I see you*. This small compliment can spark a conversation, allowing us to share stories and find common ground – a perfect icebreaker in a roomful of strangers.

Children in particular often wear shoes that spark conversation: lights, sparkles, superheroes, or rain boots with princess dresses. These choices offer a glimpse into their personalities and interests, and there's a certain magic in their freedom to wear whatever brings them joy. As we grow older, some of that magic fades, but it's worth holding on to – reminding ourselves of the freedom to wear what makes us feel good.

A simple 'I love your shoes' might have been all it took to plant a seed, inspiring a shift toward comfort and creativity in fashion. Trends often start with small acts of courage, which gain momentum as others feel seen and inspired.

High heels, too, are symbols – of freedom for some and of compliance for others. Each person's experience in their shoes is unique, and sometimes the only way to understand it is to ask.

Curiosity has a quiet power. In a world where we often assume we know how others feel, a simple question can reveal so much. The beauty lies in the smallest gestures, the ones that allow us to connect with others and bring a bit of magic back into our own lives.

Shoes That Explore Difficult Things

To wear dreams on one's feet is to begin to give a reality to one's dreams.
—Roger Vivier, the Fabergé of footwear, inventor of the stiletto

Shoes can take us across difficult terrain, both literally and emotionally. Preparing for walking through these areas can require particular types of shoes to protect us, support us, or sometimes make us faster! The quiet shoes I wore through Crumlin Hospital helped me to manage a very difficult space. It was a place I did not want to be; there was a very long corridor followed by another that led to a set of double doors into the cancer ward. Being intentional about my choice of shoe acted as a coping mechanism during these difficult times. I did love those shoes and appreciated their support during difficult times. Funnily, I was happy to wrap them up and give them away when we no longer attended Crumlin. It was like saying goodbye to an old pal; I was happy to let them off to someone else who would be happy to have them.

The picture is of me on the glass floor of the Willis Tower in Chicago. I am terrified of heights, and the stress can be seen in my clenched toes. Those shoes took me on a wonderful adventure that

The Right Shoes

summer across the USA in a camper van as we explored from Los Angeles and San Diego – visiting the Hoover Dam, Chloride, the Grand Canyon, Tucson, Tombstone (yes, it's a real place; you can visit the saloon where Doc Hollywood played cards!) – to Chicago and New York. Shoes that were kind in the heat, comfortable to walk in, and left footprints in wonderful and exciting places. I love that this photo captures a bigger picture of me at that particular moment. I didn't walk out into the window; my feet just wouldn't move out that far!

The second picture was taken in the dry, rocky ground of the Arizona desert – my name left in stones at the Apache death cave. The ground was so dry and gravelly that it was hard to leave footprints. Sometimes it's just too hard to fully leave your mark on a place, but I built my name in stones to leave behind. I wonder what story the stones have woven since? Did others wonder who Lucy was? Did little desert animals move them around? Although the desert wasn't at its hottest when I was there, it dried out my lovely shoes and caused a split. The severity of the terrain was just too much for what seemed like a sturdy shoe!

It's a reminder, isn't it, that even the things we rely on – things we assume will carry us safely and surely – aren't always invincible. Shoes splitting unexpectedly can be a little like betrayal, catching us off guard. We might feel like they 'failed' us, but in a way, they're just worn out from their time with us, the miles we've walked together.

That split can serve as a moment to pause, to think about what those shoes have been through with us, the journeys taken, and maybe even the times they protected us when we needed them most.

Stories of Others

Walking, I am listening to a deeper way. Suddenly, all my ancestors are behind me. Be still, they say. Watch and listen. You are the result of the love of thousands.
—Linda Hogan

I took a photo in my hall one day of my shoes alongside the shoes of my youngest son. It was such a stark picture of how he is grown up, no longer a child. It not only captures his growth but also brings to mind the progression of my other two older sons, tracing their steps from tiny baby shoes to sparkly, light-up sneakers to the adult shoes they now wear.

It's almost as if each pair tells about a chapter of their lives. From their first wobbly steps to confidently stepping out on their own, these shoes have been silent witnesses to all the stages in between. This has all happened right in front of me, but it is only when I saw the shoes alongside each other in the hall and stopped to take a photo that the full picture of it all hit me.

We often celebrate our first shoes with lots of photos and joy. As an adult, I have seen children in my life go from first shoes to shoes much bigger than mine, or from tiny shoes to sparkly shoes with lights to adult shoes.

We celebrate those tiny first shoes, marvelling at how small they are, filled with excitement for all the places they will take those who wear them. But there's something equally poignant about seeing those larger shoes – somehow it hits us unexpectedly. Seeing my sons' shoes measured against my own identifies the growth so very poignantly. It's the reminder that they've grown, and they're still growing, even as they start to stride beyond my reach.

There's a bittersweet magic in watching them choose their own shoes, ones that reflect their unique personalities, their choices, and their paths forward.

In the above photo of our shoes side by side, there is a wordless story, a reminder that they've gone from shoes I tied for them to shoes that will take them places beyond my view. It's a beautiful snapshot of the swift passage of time, a reminder of both the moments that were and the ones yet to come.

The Velcro shoes demonstrating how our shoes change as we age is also something that comes to mind. Baby Velcro shoes are often the first pair of shoes we buy for our little ones. Designed for tiny, developing feet, they offer several benefits: Velcro closures are quick and easy for us to fasten, especially since babies aren't yet able to tie laces. These shoes tend to be soft and flexible, allowing for natural movement while giving gentle support to growing feet. The Velcro makes them adjustable, which is useful as babies' feet grow quickly and need frequent new sizes. Plus, they're durable and stay securely on, reducing the chance of a shoe slipping off during a baby's busy day of crawling or toddling.

For elderly people, Velcro shoes also serve a very practical purpose. With age, bending down to tie laces can become challenging, especially when there is limited hand dexterity or conditions like arthritis. Velcro closures provide an accessible alternative, helping seniors maintain their independence and reducing the risk of falls due to untied laces. Many Velcro shoes for seniors are designed with comfort in mind, offering additional cushioning, support, and easy entry to accommodate potential foot issues or changes in foot shape over time.

So, Velcro shoes bookend the spectrum of life, helping out at the very beginning and once again when fine motor skills or flexibility might not be what they once were, offering ease and a sense of independence at both ends.

My lovely father-in-law was a busy, hardworking man. He loved the outdoors and working on the bog, and he was able to turn his hand to almost any job required, from putting down wooden floors in our first apartment and painting the walls to planting the lovely trees in the beautiful park in Tullamore. As he got older, there was a change in his pace, and rather than his shoes being sturdy and strong, they needed to be gentler and wrap around his feet, bringing him more comfort than speed – evidencing his need for more gentle support as he aged, his growing vulnerability and reliance on others for care. The story was starkly told through his shoes.

Shoes can tell stories about who we are and what we need as we grow up and grow older. Taking time to notice how the shoes around us change can give insight into the changing nature of our relationships.

One Of Those Days

We all have 'one of those days' stories. I was running about one day and getting ready to head out, all flustered. I stopped and looked down at my feet, as something didn't feel quite right, only to discover that I had two odd shoes on! I laughed out loud at first, then took a photo and had a firm word with myself to move forward with purpose, not just speed. At that point, I realised I needed to stop and breathe before going further.

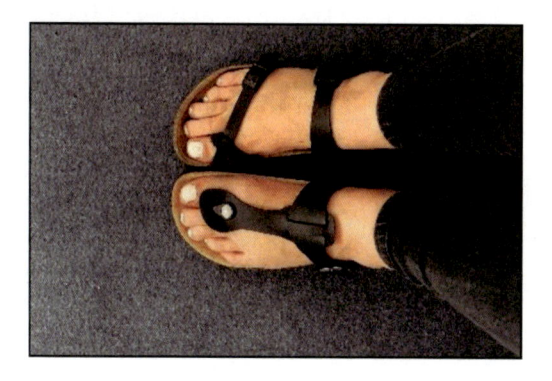

Less haste, more speed comes to mind. Taking the time to step into the moment allows us to be purposeful and steady ourselves to be fully present. This photo resonated with people I shared it with. I heard lots of crazy shoe stories about mismatched shoes! The common theme in these stories was one of unsteadiness and discombobulation that could only be remedied by a matching pair of shoes.

When I was a manager in a centre, a staff member came back to work after maternity leave. On her first day back after a busy morning, she sat down to do our handover meeting before realising she had two different boots on! After a quiet moment with a cup of tea, she headed back home to sort the shoes. Moments of overwhelm can come so easily when we have lots going on. Pausing to reset and start again allows for empathy, self-care, and a funny story for later!

Wearing mismatched shoes by accident can definitely leave you feeling off-kilter, almost like you're walking around in a surreal world where things just don't line up. Each shoe seems to demand a different kind of step, like they've got their own personalities, and that imbalance works its way up through your body, making even simple movements feel awkward. It can be a strangely humbling experience, too, as you suddenly notice that something as small as mismatched shoes can affect your balance, confidence, and focus. That little slip up keeps you off-balance all day, like your shoes are each trying to pull you in a different direction—one back home to switch them out, and the other forward, challenging you to own it.

The combination of place and shoes has a fascinating way of shaping experiences and emotions.

Right place, wrong shoes: Being in the perfect place with the wrong shoes can be frustrating. Imagine hiking a beautiful trail in dress shoes or attending a formal event in muddy sneakers. It's like you're almost there, but you're held back, uncomfortable, or unable to fully enjoy the experience. This misalignment can remind you how small details can have a big impact on even the most ideal situations. Sometimes it teaches adaptability or resilience – finding joy despite the discomfort.

Right shoes, wrong place: On the flip side, the right shoes in the wrong place might feel like carrying a piece of potential with you. You're equipped, confident, maybe even excited, but the surroundings don't match your energy. Imagine putting on your favourite running shoes only to find a city block packed with people. In this case, the shoes might feel like a reminder of where you could be – somewhere freer, more fitting for your stride.

In each scenario, the shoes feel like extensions of your intention. The 'right' shoes set you up for possibility, and when matched with the right place, they're magic. When the shoes are mismatched to the place, though, it can feel like a missed opportunity – or maybe just a reminder of the magic waiting in the right setting.

Wrong Shoes/Right Place – Right Shoes/Wrong Place

Give a girl the right shoes, and she can conquer the world.
—Marilyn Monroe

Occasionally, we encounter unfamiliar situations where navigating becomes challenging without preparation. It's crucial to align our readiness with the tasks at hand. When difficulties arise, reassessing our preparation and considering a simple change in tools or approach can often make the journey smoother.

This reminds me of the day I was wearing my slippers in the garden to survey some recent building work. Tiptoeing around, I realised a change into wellies would be much easier and more comfortable.

The Right Shoes

Sometimes when a path seems difficult, it may be that we simply do not have the right shoes; we are not prepared for the path ahead. It is smart and wise to take stock of where we are and gather some perspective to make changes that will serve us better. That day was a fun opportunity to wear my spotty wellies and slosh about in the puddles.

Powering Up!

Shoes transform your body language and attitude. They lift you physically and emotionally.
—Christian Louboutin

Shoes have the power to boost our mood and instil a sense of confidence. Imagine a pair of shoes you dream of owning – where could they take you? What feelings might they inspire? The firm sound of shoes on the ground can reinforce our self-assurance, while a bold, attention-grabbing shoe can help us stand out. We often choose special shoes for significant events to set the tone and embrace whatever the day brings.

Sometimes, they can be shoes of a brand we like, or of a particular colour or style. The song by Nancy Sinatra proclaims the power of a pair of boots: 'These boots were made for walking and that's just what they will do, one of these days these boots are gonna walk all over you!' This is a powerful message about the intent of the wearer to be seen, heard, and taken seriously.

The black shoes in the photo are one of my current favourite pairs of boots. They look like Doc Martens, but they are actually Birkenstock, 'funky but hiding the old lady', as one of my sons suggested. This picture was also taken on the gravel in UCD grounds. Walking solidly and making noise made me feel grounded and present.

The shoes below them are the ones I bought with my vouchers and student card. They are comfortable and versatile and have the Tommy Hilfiger brand, which brings its own swagger. This photo was taken at the UCD Innovation Academy.

What shoes support you in being in your power and gaining a can-do attitude? They can be different depending on the task at hand. For example, football boots can bring great solidity on the ground on a football pitch, but they could take away your power if worn to a restaurant.

Investigating the connection between wealth and shoes can lead to some interesting discussions, uncovering both the symbolic and practical aspects behind these ideas. Here are some possibilities:

Status and symbolism: Shoes have long been associated with status and social standing. Certain brands or styles of shoes are seen as symbols of wealth and success. Exploring the significance of these symbols can lead to discussions about how we perceive and signal our social status as well as the role of external markers of success in shaping self-esteem and identity.

Investment and value: Some people view shoes as investments, purchasing high-quality or designer footwear to preserve and grow their wealth. This perspective can prompt reflections on the relationship between material possessions and financial well-being and the distinction between value and worth.

Mindful consumption: On the other hand, pursuing wealth through material possessions like expensive shoes can also be seen as a form of conspicuous consumption. Conversations around this can explore questions of intentionality, sustainability, and the alignment of spending habits with personal values and long-term goals.

Entrepreneurship and innovation: For some industries related to fashion or footwear, shoes may represent opportunities for entrepreneurship and innovation. Discussions could focus on strategies for leveraging creativity, identifying market trends, and building a brand in competitive industries.

Financial literacy and planning: Exploring the metaphor of shoes in the context of wealth can also serve as a springboard for discussions about financial literacy and planning. Just as different types of shoes serve different purposes, we can learn to diversify and manage our financial portfolios effectively, understanding the importance of risk management and long-term planning.

Generosity and philanthropy: Lastly, the concept of wealth and shoes can be linked to notions of generosity and philanthropy. Conversations might explore how we can use wealth, whether material or otherwise, to positively impact our communities and the world. This could involve discussions about charitable giving, volunteerism, or socially responsible investing.

By exploring the intersection of wealth and shoes through conversations, we can gain insights into our relationship with money, success, and personal values. It offers an opportunity to reflect on the role of material possessions in our lives and to consider how we can align our financial goals with our broader aspirations for fulfilment and well-being.

Bare Feet

One shoe can change your life.
—Cinderella

Sometimes kicking off our shoes and enjoying what is around us is what we need. This photo shows me and my family sprawled around the room after a busy day trekking around Eindhoven. I love this photo; I took it after we spent the day doing tourist things and exploring the city. We were all tired and needed a little down time before heading for dinner. It represents togetherness, adventures, and ease in each other's company.

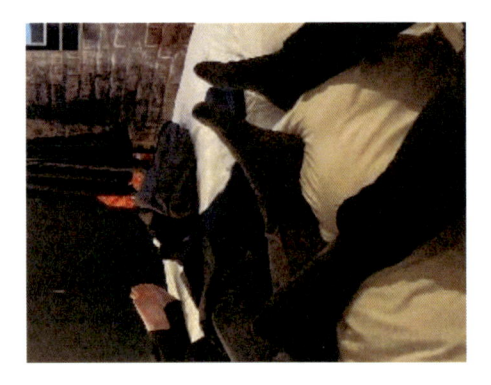

The second one was taken on the Aran Islands, where we spent a short break with friends when my son was ill. It was a time to settle, recharge, and reconnect to what is important. I remember the feeling of my feet solidly on the ground in this wild and beautiful space, and I am grateful for the experience of bare feet and connection. Taking time at a lovely location with our shoes off, standing firmly on the ground and feeling the earth beneath our feet or the sand between our toes, can connect us back to our best selves. I love these photos, where I'm taking in the beauty around me and feeling the ground so solidly beneath my feet. It was freeing, grounding, and beautiful – such an easily accessible, simple gift to myself.

We all wear shoes, but can we use our choice of shoes to create flow, purpose, and intention, supporting us in living our values? The choice of shoes for your day can support building your mental fitness. Tracy Dennis-Tiwary speaks of the wisdom of anxiety – listening to our own wisdom and balancing the concern with the possible gains. We do difficult things to build our antifragility, the concept that we work hard stretching outside our comfort zone to do new and difficult things to learn how to master doing difficult things. We build our antifragility by testing it and making it stronger, similar to our immune system learning how to fight germs by fighting germs.

Selecting the right shoes can help us create a sense of flow, aligning with the terrain we're navigating and the impression we wish to make. Do we prefer to make an entrance with loud, attention-grabbing footwear, or do we choose a quieter approach?

The approach we choose also matters when dealing with the elements, such as when we decide to wear flip-flops on scorching surfaces or sturdy walking shoes for rugged mountain paths.

By thoughtfully choosing shoes to navigate the path ahead, can we equip ourselves to journey through life with greater purpose and significance?

The absence of shoes might reflect poverty or a deliberate lifestyle choice, each carrying its own narrative. The stories are limitless. Cultivating curiosity and empathy opens doors to growth, learning, and enriched dialogue. Delving into the idea of bare feet introduces a deeper dimension to our discussions, contrasting with the symbolism and tales tied to wearing shoes. These include:

Freedom and authenticity: Bare feet can symbolise freedom and authenticity. They strip away the layers and barriers, allowing us to connect more directly with our environment and ourselves. This can lead to discussions about embracing vulnerability and authenticity in personal interactions.

Grounding and connection: Walking barefoot connects us more intimately with the ground beneath us, fostering a sense of grounding and connection to the earth. This can prompt reflections on finding grounding practices in daily life and cultivating a deeper connection to our surroundings.

Sensitivity and awareness: Without the cushioning and protection of shoes, bare feet become more sensitive to textures, temperatures, and sensations. This heightened awareness can spark conversations about mindfulness and tuning into subtle cues in our environment and relationships.

Vulnerability and courage: Walking barefoot in certain environments requires vulnerability and courage, especially if the terrain is rough or unfamiliar. This can serve as a metaphor for stepping outside our comfort zone and embracing discomfort as a catalyst for growth.

Simplicity and minimalism: Bare feet represent simplicity and minimalism, shedding unnecessary layers and attachments. This can inspire discussions about simplifying our life, letting go of excess, and focusing on what truly matters.

Incorporating the concept of bare feet into our conversations can provide a rich opportunity for self-reflection and exploration. It invites us to consider the ways in which we engage with the world around us and offers insights into our values, fears, and aspirations. Whether discussing the freedom of authenticity or the vulnerability of exposure, bare feet offer a powerful metaphor for personal growth and transformation.

Walk in My Shoes for a Day: The Power of Empathy

Rather than walking in your shoes, I need to learn how to listen to the story you tell about what it's like in your shoes and believe you.
—Brené Brown, Atlas of the Heart

The idea of walking in someone else's shoes to understand them better and empathise with them doesn't sit right with me. When we try to 'walk in someone else's shoes', we inevitably interpret their experience through our own filters, perspectives, and biases. True understanding comes not from assuming we know what someone else feels but from walking alongside them – being present, curious, and open to their interpretation of their experience. Walking alongside someone for a part of their journey and believing what they tell us, building a shared experience, is much more fruitful for connection, empathy, and healing.

By offering empathy and actively listening, we give others the space to express how they feel in their own words without imposing our own interpretations. This helps build deeper connections and fosters an environment where the person feels heard and supported rather than judged or misunderstood. This approach emphasises that understanding is a shared journey where curiosity and belief in the other's experience are key to truly connecting.

To wear another person's shoes also takes something from them at a time they may most need it.

Auditing Our Shoe Collection

I still have my feet on the ground – I just wear better shoes.
—Oprah Winfrey

What arsenal of support do you have in your shoe collection? Each pair can offer something unique just by being worn. For instance, the type of shoes worn at school might provide a comforting sense of belonging. I once observed a group of teenagers engaged in a peculiar contest: who had the most worn-out shoes. Some of their shoes were barely hanging on to their soles. Intrigued, I dug deeper and discovered a fascinating story. Wearing these tattered shoes carried a certain status – they symbolised a victorious struggle against authority, a challenge to teachers, and the thrill of causing a stir. Interestingly, each teen admitted to having a new pair at home, reserved for everywhere but school. There was a delicate balance in keeping the shoes as damaged as possible without them falling apart, as new shoes would end the game.

I spoke with the leader of a conference recently during the coffee break. She was very tall and wore very high shoes. She asked if I thought her shoes were high enough, as she had higher ones. To her, there was power in higher shoes that brought status and courage.

If you look at your own shoe collection, what does each pair say to you? Do they fit with you now, or do they carry stories of nostalgia, achievement, or overstretch?

The stories your shoes tell offer a fun way to explore your unique perspective on the world. They invite you on a journey of self-discovery as you reflect on your footwear. No one else in the world possesses a shoe collection quite like yours, with the same intentions, purposes, and journeys behind it. This reflects each person's individuality, and while we might share similar shoes with others, our collections are curated with a distinct intent, vision, and purpose that mirrors our uniqueness.

This offers a chance to embark on a journey of self-discovery, using a simple everyday item to reflect on how you see yourself, understand how others perceive you, and explore ways to alter your approach, shift your mindset, and embrace greater intentionality in your life.

Are you interested in finding out how?

You cannot act like flip flops and expect to be treated like Louboutins.
—Anon

Let's pause for thought at this point. Some self-reflection might be useful. I have set out some questions for you to consider as you take the time to review how these ideas impact you and how you can make them real.

Think about the emotions evoked – the impact on your nervous system that each of the questions elicits. See what surprises you. But first you need to own your own footprints!

Owning Your Own Footsteps

Footsteps serve as a powerful metaphor for life's journey, shaping who you are. Each step symbolises the choices you make, the paths you take, and the experiences you encounter. The places you walk, your manner of walking, and the directions you choose reflect your values, intentions, and personality. Much like how certain shoes can reveal aspects of your identity, your footsteps map out a personal journey, showcasing persistence, exploration, or even hesitation. As you move through the world, they leave a lasting imprint, both physically and metaphorically.

Physically, different shoes change how you walk:

Comfort: A well-fitting, comfortable shoe allows you to walk more naturally and confidently, while ill-fitting or uncomfortable shoes can alter your gait, make you cautious, or cause pain that slows you down.

Purpose: Shoes designed for specific activities (like running shoes, hiking boots, or formal shoes) change your stride and how you navigate environments. Running shoes, for instance, promote efficiency and speed, while heavy boots may make you tread more deliberately.

Mood and confidence: Wearing shoes you love or feel good in can boost confidence, making your steps more purposeful and assured.

In contrast, shoes you're uncomfortable with might make you feel hesitant or self-conscious.

Metaphorically, your shoes symbolise different phases or mindsets in life. Choosing practical shoes could reflect a focus on responsibility, while something bold or adventurous might reflect your readiness for new challenges. It aligns with the idea that the shoes you wear are sometimes the ones you need for where you're headed in life.

Self-Audit

The journey with your shoes could allow you to audit the shoes you have, the shoes you need, and the shoes that serve you well.

Gathering information to understand your unique narrative can enable you to drive it purposely and feel more connected to self and others.

Let's ask the beautiful question posed by Mary Oliver in her poem 'Summer Day' (I have emphasised the 'with your' part of the question to focus on you when reflecting on the question):

What is it you plan to do

WITH YOUR

one wild and precious life?

The following questions will prompt you in your self audit. For the downloadable workbook containing these questions, please reach out to Lucy on lucy.cronly@gmail.com.

What story do your shoes tell?
Have a look at your feet and the shoes you chose for today. Tell yourself the story about the shoes you are currently wearing. Where did you buy them? When did you buy them? What did you envisage when you picked them up?

What shoes do you wish you had?
What shoes do you want to have? These are not necessarily the ones you need, but they draw you and offer something. What could that be? What would they bring into your life?

How did your shoes come into your life?
Was it a special occasion? A practical purpose? Did you see them on someone else and want to emulate what you saw?

Where do they bring you well?
Where are the places that you would feel most comfortable wearing these shoes? What extra would they offer to the event or occasion? What landscape or terrain do each of your pairs of shoes like best?

What impact does your choice of shoes have on others?

What comment do others make about your shoes? Do you have a particular pair that draws comments? Is there a theme to comments made about your choice of shoes?

Where would they not be welcome?

Where would your current shoes not serve you well? Think about the earlier pictures. Although slippers are perfect at home, cosy by the fire, they are very uncomfortable on a building site. Where could a bad choice of shoe change the perception of you?

What shoes are you most comfortable wearing in what space?

What is your current favourite pair of shoes? What was your last favourite pair?

The Right Shoes

Who could buy you a pair of shoes you would love without discussing them with you first?

If someone was to spend a day in your shoes, what would they learn about you?

If your shoes were an introduction in a room, what would they say?

Gathering the Wisdom: Shoe Stories

I sent out a questionnaire to some people I thought might be interested in contributing their thoughts to the book (see Appendix 1).

I was so delighted that I received the following replies; they add so much value to the story. You will see how the idea resonated differently for each person, yet there were common themes of finding joy, accessing safety, and establishing a sense of identity evident in the answers presented.

Each person chose how they wanted to be identified, whether it was by their family, profession, or outlook on life. I left this wide open for each person to decide.

Thank you to each contributor for your thoughts, reflections, and encouragement to get this book done. I appreciate each of you walking with me on the journey.

Eimear

We spoke one evening and over the course of our conversation I shared the idea for 'The Right Shoes' Talking about how it could be a useful everyday item that is all around us that could take measure of who we are, who we want to be and who we spend our time with. The idea that noticing shoes and being curious about them could offer a narrative.

We met again the following week and Eimear shared a story about a birthday party she had attended the previous weekend. She arrived to the house and the shoes of both parents and the child who was celebrating their birthday were sitting together in the hall. She saw a story in the shoes sitting there together, the mothers' shoes, the fathers' shoes and the shoes of the child sitting cosily between them. There was a sadness in the visual as the parents were splitting up and these shoes would not sit in the hall together anymore. The narrative of the family told so strikingly in their shoes sitting in the hall. Our conversation the previous week had added the layer of noticing the story offered by the shoes sitting in the hall.

Reflection

It is the power of ordinary things, shoes sitting in the hall weaving a narrative for a family being noticed by a visitor to the house. It offered an opportunity for empathy and kindness for the family on their life journey.

Eddie Molloy

Eddie describes himself as a man who throughout his life has always planned ahead. *'I worry too much,' he says. 'At eighty-three, I worry about big things in front of me, end of life and quality of life. My career is behind me and I am grateful for the success and opportunities it brought, but it is not anymore how I identify myself. Now I am seeking to strike a better balance with worry, passing the baton for the future to younger generations, satisfied with my contributions. I am in a good place, I am older, and I understand the importance of seeking the joy around me in adventures to visit people who matter to me, enjoying sport, and reaping the rewards of worry of bygone days, which allowed me to plan well for these golden years.'*

I sent Eddie my questionnaire, and he rang me, conveying his answers. The conversation took about thirty minutes and was full of insight and reflection. I have always looked to Eddie's wisdom at different points in my life. He is my maternal uncle, full of kindness and compassion, a man of his word who sees things and looks to make them better – an inspirational man who has provided me with a scaffold of safety and given me courage to do brave things.

Eddie spoke about the choices we make about shoes. Choices are not always available to him and his contemporaries; comfort is more important than anything else, and this reflects his age and mobility. Managing foot health is a major concern for octogenarians, and finding shoes that bring comfort is a quest. He spoke about a local shoe shop that was doing great business in comfortable shoes when he visited, where he was asked if he had been sent by the physiotherapist – which indeed he had. A story of collaboration too!

He also told the story of how when he was a young boy, many children in Dublin's Dominick Street didn't have shoes and went barefoot all year round. The *Evening Herald* newspaper ran a boot fund to buy shoes for children in the city. He pointed out that there is a privilege in having a choice of shoes.

'I believe myself to be kind,' Eddie said, and this is something I can wholeheartedly confirm. There are a few stories that he holds as having a strong influence on him. He remembers a small child calling to his house and his mother opening the door. A child not known to his mother was there, a boy aged four or five from a family of six or seven children. His mother, my granny, brought the child in, cleaned and fed him, took out her sewing machine, made him a pair of trousers, and sent him on his way.

Again as a young child, he recalls, there was a time of flooding in Italy when the Red Cross collected items to send out for relief. His dad, my granddad, had just bought new shoes. Granddad packed up his new shoes to send. Eddie asked him why he was sending his new shoes, and Granddad matter-of-factly said there was no point in sending old shoes.

Eddie spoke about his dad keeping the family shod. He had a shoe repair kit, and he re-soled and re-heeled shoes on a Saturday evening when he was off work, cutting out the leather to bring new life to tired shoes.

The final story began on a Sunday morning when Eddie dropped his wife to Mass on Temple Road. There was a click-clack of high heels that caught his attention; they sounded like high heels that were too big, like shoes worn by a small child. A young Black woman was heading for the Luas tram, dressed in a frilly pink dress and pulling along a small suitcase. There was a sense of something out of place; what was this young woman doing out like this on a Sunday morning? Was she in danger? Eddie had a sense of something amiss and afterwards felt that he should have checked with her to make sure she was okay. He was left with a memory of inappropriate shoes and an uneasy feeling.

Eddie thinks shoes could be used as a useful segue into conversations. In his own work, he used musical instruments, asking people, '*If you were a musical instrument, what would you be?*' This gave him a wonderful point of entry into deeper conversation, where people were less defensive as they considered how instruments work together and the features of the instruments that gave interesting insights. Eddie proposes these questions: *What goes with shoes? Where do they fit in? And putting them into a wider context, what complements shoes?*

Eddie's answer to someone buying him shoes that he would love was an adamant, definite no! The shoes must fit and be comfortable. He thought the question was about someone he loved buying him shoes and said it really didn't matter how much someone loved him; it was all about practicality.

We chatted about the misinterpretation of the question, which on reflection may have been a little unclear, but still the answer was no. Comfort could only be determined by trying them on, and this was not negotiable. The importance of comfort while in motion is a crucial support in Eddie's day.

The question about admiring someone's shoes brought a story about a recent event Eddie had attended. Although Eddie thought this question was more related to women's shoes, his observations related to men. There was a pair of shoes that drew his attention; they were red-and-cream leather and looked custom made, worn by a wealthy man. There was another pair that were black, shiny, and pointy, and they were struggling to contain the man's feet in them. Both pairs looked uncomfortable but expensive, designed as a status symbol and for putting the best foot forward.

Eddie's plan for the day he answered the questions was to go between his slippers and the joy of the wonderful shoes his physiotherapist had recommended and he'd bought locally. From comfort to comfort, so very important to him.

We spoke about shoes around the world, and he told me about his time in the Franciscans. When he joined, he had open-toed sandals made for him by a fellow monk who was a cobbler. He wore them everywhere, regardless of the weather, which aligned with the vow of poverty taken by the monks.

It was a privilege to hear so many beautiful, heartfelt stories and share this conversation with Eddie.

Mandy Lowbridge

Mandy lives in Tullamore. She has three grown up children and is a grandmother to three amazing granddaughters. Mandy declares herself to be addicted to the joy of new shoes.

What shoes are you wearing today?
Today, runners. I feel like I need comfort and support.

How do shoes make you feel?
I think shoes can determine our mood and feelings; when I wear new shoes, I feel like the bee's knees; many people make analogies using shoes.

Could someone else buy you shoes you would love?
Yes. My daughter absolutely could buy my shoes. She bought my Doc Martens. She just seems to inherently know how and what type of shoes make me feel good. It's like a special connection we have.

What shoe story would you like to share?
I had an uncle called Pat Joe, whose shoes were always polished and you could see your face in them. As a kid I once asked him why he polished them all the time, and he said, 'The state of a man's shoes are the measure of him.' I never saw him in unpolished shoes.

My dad used to say I was like Imelda Marcos with all the shoes I owned. I had fighting shoes, which he said were Doc Martens. When I went out for the night, I wore ankle breakers [high heels]. When I was really busy doing errands, it was runners, because he said I was always on the run.

What is your current favourite pair of shoes?
Converse boots, not as aggressive as Docs but sturdy enough to make me feel safe.

Reflection

Mandy's stories reflect her relationship with her dad, her uncle, and her daughter. Having different shoes for different places and tasks reflects her different moods and purposes. The fact that she has shoes that help her feel safe and that they offer different levels of safety depending on what is needed offers some lovely insights into her self-care and her understanding of what she needs. We chatted together after she sent me her thoughts, and she said she had really enjoyed the task and questions, as they gave her the opportunity to think about her connection with important people in her life. Using shoes as a segue allowed her to access some lovely memories and knowledge about herself.

Susan Buckley

Susan lives in the lovely seaside town of Bray. She has two amazing grown-up children and three grandchildren. Her current favourite shoes are gold boots.

Susan says, *'I'm fifty-four this year, and back in January, I saw a pair of boots on the Una Healy website – gold cowboy boots. I thought they were just magnificent. I looked at them on and off and battled with myself as to whether or not I was too old for such flashy footwear, and could I justify the sixty euros. After about three months, I was given thirty euros for my birthday, so feck it, I got them, and I love them, and people admire them, and just looking at them on my feet makes me so happy.'* This joyful story reflects Susan's uniqueness and her sense of adventure and fun.

Susan speaks poignantly about shoes as a sense of identity and how wearing shoes makes you stand out when there is a strong desire to fit in. At points in one's life, she says, this can be difficult to manage. As a child of the seventies and eighties, she often didn't have a choice of shoes, and access to fast fashion wasn't available. Practicality and economics often led to shoes that didn't tell a story that felt good and could expose the wearer to teasing by other kids, especially when their sense of identity and their wonderful uniqueness had not been embraced. Funny thing is that what is highly trendy and fashionable one year can be laughed at the following year, which is especially tough for children and young adults.

Reflecting on whether someone could buy shoes for her, Susan says, *'No, I think I'd have to discuss it with them first. One of my feet is slightly bigger than the other – one is a six and the other a six and a half – so I have to try everything on to figure out which size I get.*

'I bought a pair of sliders for my sister once, and was sorely disappointed when I realised she couldn't wear them because they didn't have a toe post, something she couldn't do without and I should have known about her, as I've known her all my life . . . and here we were in our fifties, discovering something we hadn't shared before.'

This answer gave me pause for reflection. Sometimes we think we know someone, and with familiarity we can think we know more than we do. This story reminded me of the importance of checking things out with even those very familiar to us.

Susan speaks about shoes as a segue into meaningful conversation. *'I find it fascinating how the symbolism of shoes has struck chords with people over the years. When Catherine Corless broke the story of seven hundred ninety-six babies' bodies in a septic tank in Tuam in 2014, there was a call for an inquest, and one of the demonstrations tied hundreds of pairs of babies' shoes to a railing, one for every baby thrown away like rubbish. When I saw it, it was a punch in the guts; the symbolism was huge.' Indeed, the symbolism allowed a story to be told so poignantly without any words, opening up a societal conversation about valuing human life and dignity.*

There is a story in a worn shoe, a journey taken by someone, Susan says. A story of places they have been and things they have done, giving a sense of their identity. Identity was a recurring theme in this dialogue and opened up a meaningful interaction with Susan that created so much food for thought.

Nigel Cronly

My spouse, Nigel, is an engineer and the service manager of a semiconductor company in Ireland.

Look down at your feet. What story do your shoes tell today?
Skechers slip-ons. Easy to get on and comfortable. These days, sadly, this is my priority when picking what shoes to wear :-(. I think if they were to tell a story, it would be that sometimes we make decisions based on need rather than desire.

What do you think about using shoes as a segue into meaningful conversations?
I think this is a great idea. You can tell a lot about a person by their shoes. Shoes see the world in a real and tangible way, always moving.

Do you know someone who could buy you shoes that you love without discussing them with you? Who would this be and why?
My wonderful wife. She knows me so well; she could buy me shoes in a heartbeat. I think when you really know someone, you know what they like and what they don't like ;-) .

Have you ever admired someone's shoes and been surprised by the story behind the shoes? Can you share the story?

I once met a guy who had a pair of flip-flops made out of old tyres he bought in Mexico. He said they were very comfy and only cost him twenty dollars. What he liked about them was that they were made for him and no other pair would be exactly the same.

What's your shoe plan for today or tomorrow and why?

I plan to wear my DMs, but I will probably end up wearing my slip-on Skechers.

Additionally, if you have a personal shoe story you would like to share, I would be thrilled to include it in the book.

Shoes can be a great source of happiness. When I was fourteen, I got a pair of brown flight boots that I loved. I remember as a teenager wearing these always made me happy. Wearing them always would make my day happier. Sometimes it's the little things that get you through your day. Shoes are magical; they move you through life and hand you off to the next pair when they wear out, which no doubt will be very different. Sometimes you wear the shoes you really want, sometimes the shoes you really need; the sad part is that they are not always the same shoes.

Reflection

Shoes are such a fascinating metaphor for life – Nigel's reflection captures that beautifully. They carry stories of where he has been, what he has prioritised, and what he hopes to do next. From the flight boots that made him feel happy to the well-worn, practical slip-ons that reflect the here and now, shoes can symbolise so much more than just fashion. Nigel's answers reveal that it is often in those little decisions, like what shoes to wear, that we find the bigger picture of our daily journey. They also give a glimpse into his relationship with his wife (me!) and how he feels seen by her.

Nigel's answers highlight and support the idea that something as everyday as shoes can carry deep meaning about identity, comfort, and adaptation. His reflections on shoes hint that he is someone who sees beyond the surface, appreciating the deeper connections between everyday objects and the human experience. He can see shoes not just as practical items but as personal symbols – of comfort, movement, and even identity. He notices and values how small details, like a pair of shoes, can carry a story or a history.

Colette Doris

Colette lives in Mountshannon, County Clare, and runs the Mountain Studio, where she teaches yoga to groups and couples as well as one-to-one. She is also a practicing life coach with neuroscience, exploring the connection between the mind and the body.

Her interest in the connection between the head, heart, and gut, through thirty years of teaching, has led her to run hour-long yoga nidra sessions, allowing rejuvenation and release to bring greater health to the whole person as well as lessening anxiety and improving sleep.

She says, *'My shoes today are Crocs, white Crocs. I love white shoes; they give me a sense of brightness, cheerfulness, and remind me of my childhood. I had glass dress-up slippers, which were sparkly, and I've never forgotten them.*

'This made me giggle! I often converse with my husband, Tif, re his shoes, as he keeps buying small, narrow Chinese-made shoes online, which don't fit, and we end up having a laugh about them.

The Right Shoes

'But yes, I do talk and admire other people's shoes a lot. For me, there's only so far I've got discussing shoes, but I'd say they have the potential for leading to discussions on grounding, self-esteem, boots-under-the-table themes – that is, settling in as a person to family, relationship, or place.

'I think any of my six children could buy me boots or shoes that I would wear; they often borrow them, so we share taste in style and colour. My close friend Audrey is another person who could and has given me shoes I like and they fit. She's known me for thirty years and has a great eye. We are very close, so she's attuned to my tastes and needs.

'I often admire others' shoes, but to be honest, right now I can't think of a surprising story behind them. Except for my son Reuben, who is now twenty-seven. He had a girlfriend from ages fifteen to twenty, and it was hard for us all but him most importantly when they finished. He was a wearer of hurling boots, Converse, Vans, and runners. His ex bought him for his birthday a pair of brown leather Doc Martens shoes, which he loved. They have been in the hall since he went to the US two years ago, waiting to be repaired. They are incredibly beaten up. So far two cobblers have opted not to get involved. Back in the hall, our brown Labrador, Billy, who adores Reuben, often sleeps with his head on these shoes.

'Tomorrow I am going to Westport to stay in Knockranny House, to see my son Aaron and his girlfriend for the night. I plan to wear my new white calf-length cowboy boots! As Nancy Sinatra sang, "these boots are made for walkin'"; that's just what I'll do. "One of these days these boots are gonna walk all over you." More the sentiment as in determination and fire. Get up and go. With a bit of style!

Reflection

The themes of identity, connection, and how Colette likes to show up in the world come through in such a lovely way through her writing. The way Colette's friend and children are able to find shoes for her clearly shows how connected she feels to them and how attuned they are to her tastes and needs.

White, bright, and sparkly shoes paint such a lovely picture and really do mirror how Colette shows up. The connection to childhood is poignant too.

Buying shoes online is a tricky one, given the importance of comfort over style. Sometimes what we think will work just doesn't when we try them on.

The story of Billy missing his pal and sleeping on his shoes evokes the emotion of sadness over missing someone and staying connected in a small but meaningful way.

And then Colette was off to Westport in her fabulous new white cowboy boots, full of determination and fire with a blast of get-up-and-go. Hope you had a wonderful visit!

Lynn Roberts

Lynn lives in sunny Tucson, Arizona, where she finds a fulfilling life balance with family, friends, and running a small business.

Look down at your feet. What story do your shoes tell today?

My shoe choice of the day is a strappy platform slip-on sandal by Reef. They are super comfortable, have that beachy vibe, and I get compliments on them regularly. I let my hair dry in soft waves, throw on a pair of chino shorts and a T-shirt, and feel that quintessential summer relaxed mood.

What do you think about using shoes as a segue into meaningful conversations?

When I see someone, male or female, in an interesting pair of shoes, I will compliment them. It is one of the few articles of clothing that people feel comfortable discussing and seems less stigmatised than drawing attention to a top or a pair of pants. People appreciate the compliment and will often share a smile and more about their shoe choice.

Do you know someone who could buy you shoes that you love without discussing them with you? Who would this be and why?

There are three men in my life who could choose sneakers for me that I would love: my brother and two of my sons. They are very perceptive people, and we have a shared love of comfortable and trendy sneakers.

Additionally, if you have a personal shoe story you would like to share, I would be thrilled to include it in the book.

As a young child, I can remember the importance my mother put on shoes each season. Every spring, my mother would take me to get new white strappy sandals with a flat sole. These would be my shoes throughout the summer. We would drive up to meet my grandmother at the retail store where she worked, and Mom would pick a new pair of sandals for me. They looked so clean and new, and I was always excited to get my new pair. Throughout the season, we would apply polish and buff them until they looked almost new again.

As children, my mom would take my brother and me to get new pairs of sneakers from a discount sneaker store near our home. My mother would select canvas Keds with the white rubber toe and sole, in red or navy blue for me. As I got a bit older, I was allowed to choose my sneakers myself, and I went for the cool Chuck Taylor Converse All Stars. I remember when I was twelve (late 1970s) being allowed to select a high-top multicolour pair with panels in purple, green, red, and yellow —what they call colour block today. I felt so fabulous in those sneakers!

Once I graduated from college in the late 1980s, I needed to step up my shoe game to work in the business world. At that time, pointy-toed pumps – or stilettos, if you dared – was de rigueur for office women. These high heels had the added advantage of making me taller, and as I was a woman in a mostly male office, it gave me greater self-confidence. I wore pumps in neutral colours for regular workdays, but I also had red-and-purple suede stilettos for Fridays, when my girlfriends and I would go out for lunch and then maybe out for drinks after work. Paired with a pencil skirt and crisp blouse, I felt like I owned it!

Reflection

The narrative that shoes can evoke is so present in Lynn's writing. The rituals of childhood around shoes so clearly speak to connection and preparation for the upcoming season. The story of the annual trip to get sandals and keeping them tip top for the season paints such an air of excitement for the summer ahead. Loving the newness of shoes and what their purchase will bring is seen in the new shoes for summer, Lynn branching out to picking her own shoes, and the new shoes that came with a new budding career. I love the Friday shoes, showing the fun and excitement of the upcoming weekend. High heels giving extra height and making Lynn feel like she 'owned it' just made me smile. Shoes to set yourself up well are reflected throughout Lynn's writing. I can picture you, Lynn, strutting your stuff, holding your own! Knowing who can buy you shoes, sharing a common joy with others, and feeling seen is such a gift of connection.

Lynn writes about noticing other people's shoes, noting that it can be a point of connection and conversation. As she said, these are compliments that can be offered and accepted comfortably, a possible segue into conversation, sometimes with a complete stranger.

Themes of connection and identity flow through Lynn's writing with glimmers of the joy that shoes can bring. Lynn creates purpose by setting herself up with new shoes, bought with intention, for new adventures ahead.

Orla Kelly (publisher)
Look down at your feet. What story do your shoes tell today?

I bought these stylish platform runners at the beginning of COVID. Somehow I sensed I'd need firm support under my foot, something to elevate me off the ground but keep me balanced, and these shoes have stood the test of time. Instead of having a negative association with COVID, they remind me that I invested in myself during that time and gave myself the support I needed. Did I think it would be my shoes that made this difference? Never, but to this day I still won't part with them and wear them on occasion.

What do you think about using shoes as a segue into meaningful conversations?

It is so noninvasive and a wonderful way to start a conversation – an icebreaker.

Do you know someone who could buy you shoes that you love without discussing them with you? Who would this be and why?

No one. No matter how good they look, if I don't feel comfortable in them or have anything to wear with them, I won't wear them. I have gone shopping with friends and ended up impulse-buying or being persuaded that shoes were great for me or of great value only to give them to charity shops.

Have you ever admired someone's shoes and been surprised by the story behind the shoes? Can you share the story?

Not yet, but I am always open to a good story!

What's your shoe plan for today or tomorrow and why?

I am meeting a client later, so I will put on my black boots. They are stylish, comfortable, a block sturdy heel, just enough to give me height and stop me from wobbling so I can walk steady with confidence.

Additionally, if you have a personal shoe story you would like to share, I would be thrilled to include it in the book.

I remember pulling ankle boots from the bottom of the cupboard in the semi darkness and putting them on. I had felt tired that morning but felt I must be coming down with something like vertigo, as my balance felt very off, and I was unsteady on my feet going downstairs for breakfast. I had such a busy morning with school drop-offs and errands, one of which was food shopping. I hadn't improved much all morning, and it was only when I was at the store's checkout leaning on my trolley that I looked down and gasped in horror. I was wearing two completely different ankle boots – one platform and one narrow block; no wonder my balance was off. They were also different colours, albeit dark colours – one black and one dark green! I couldn't help but giggle after initially being mortified. I am sure I got some amused looks, but being on a mission and a short timeline for shopping, I missed out on any strange looks. Part of me hoped everyone else was too busy and caught up in their own thoughts to notice.

Reflection

Orla writes about her need for support and about how the shoes she bought during COVID offered style, balance, and some elevation. Her connection to these shoes as something she did to invest in herself at a difficult time is fascinating. Doing this unknowingly is helpful, but to do it knowing that you are setting yourself up to feel supported at a tough time and then being able to access that feeling through choosing your shoes is powerful.

Her clear statement that she 'won't wear' shoes that are not comfortable and don't fit her current style evidences that she has knowledge of herself in the bank, allowing her space to consider what will be useful and purposeful.

The shoes she planned to wear that day were chosen to give her confidence. Setting out with intent, Orla knows what she needs and how she wants to show up.

Orla provides a great story highlighting the need for balance and to be well connected to the ground by calling attention to the unbalanced feeling of two mismatched shoes. Sometimes it's not that we are in the wrong place; it's that we are wearing the wrong shoes. Life can be so very busy sometimes, and in trying to get things done quickly, taking a moment to set ourselves up well can really help. It's such a relatable story!

Next Steps

It's not about the shoes, it's what you do in them.
—Michael Jordan

If you have taken the self-audit in the previous section, you will no doubt be surprised by what comes up regarding emotions, memories, and impact. If you haven't taken it, now would be a really good time before you continue.

The self-audit is a fun, practical way to evaluate how you manage yourself and key relationships. We all wear shoes, so they are an everyday object that can create space for understanding our own uniqueness and open conversations.

'Talk to someone' is advice often given, but it assumes people know who to approach and how to start a conversation. It also presumes an understanding of setting boundaries and taking personal responsibility – skills that can be developed for a better life. This involves:

→ Exploring personal values and which ones we want to nurture, like trust and kindness, and recognizing our responsibility to live according to these values.

→ Focusing on a specific skill with exercises that delve into its impact and how to harness it to become our best selves.

The concept of using shoes as a metaphor to initiate conversations is expanding, thanks to feedback and shared wisdom from others. I am always eager for meaningful conversations that promote learning and growth. In my role as a coach, I frequently encounter recurring themes, which I've organised into areas of interest. While these areas often intersect, they offer a framework for understanding common patterns I've observed in my work.

Habits Every Day – Embracing Choice

What is a habit, and what is a choice? Have you stopped to think of the difference?

Examine your habits and cultivate ones that resonate with your core values and priorities. By breaking habits into a series of micro-choices, you create a framework to assess your decision-making abilities in alignment with your goals. Though breaking a habit can be challenging, disrupting these automatic routines or micro-choices can lead to meaningful change.

Changing your shoes and being more intentional in your footwear can be a useful interruption. Or change your route; we have all driven or walked somewhere on automatic pilot, not really noticing our surroundings. Think of it as your trip to the supermarket, where you run around and grab the things you want, knowing where they all are. Then you pop in some evening, and the place has changed. This happened to me a few weeks ago. Suddenly, I needed to be more purposeful, move slower, and be more aware of my movements and surroundings.

Listening Skills

The way we communicate with ourselves and others can reveal much about the complex scenarios we create. By examining how we interpret others, strive to form meaningful connections, and navigate the array of voices around us, we can make decisions that work best for us. Simply taking words at face value can cause us to overlook the subtle nuances in what we say, what we mean, and the filters we apply when interpreting others' words. Being curious can offer the opportunity to ask questions and seek clarification to understand each other better.

The realisation that we listen to our own voices (inner and outer) all day, every day, and have heard every word we have ever said also calls us to task. How do we speak to ourselves?

We can use our shoes as an opportunity to reflect on how we listen to others and consider how others listen to us. Think about the impact of your footsteps; who is happy to hear them? What do your footsteps bring? Love, empathy, support, anger, frustration?

Knowing how we show up in situations can allow us to make different choices and change to something that better aligns with who we want to be.

Being Wholehearted

When it comes to living wholeheartedly, Brené Brown has done extensive work around living to our values, being brave, and holding clear boundaries. What benefit is there to embracing wholeheartedness? Taking the wholehearted approach to living our lives means we can choose the shoes we want to wear, be clear about how we want to show up, and allow others to do the same.

If we are on the football pitch of life, wearing our football boots and playing our best, we can be more aware of how we interpret criticism. Who will support us with constructive criticism and advice? Whose advice should we not heed?

This empowers us to make decisions that truly benefit us, enabling us to set healthy boundaries, identify meaningful relationships, and choose where to invest our time and energy for growth.

Knowing Your Purpose – Finding Your Why

Knowing your purpose involves reflecting on what is important to you and what drives you. You can align your actions with a deeper sense of meaning by identifying your core values, passions, and motivations. Your purpose serves as a guide during both good and challenging times, helping you stay focused and resilient. It is rooted in what fulfils you, the impact you want to have, and the legacy you want to leave behind. Regular reflection, setting intentional goals, and staying open to growth are key to living a purposeful life. The insightful work of Simon Sinek is a useful framework for this thinking.

Be purposeful in your actions, align with your core values, and understand your motivations. This approach provides clarity during challenging times by keeping the bigger picture in mind and enhances your capacity for joy and gratitude during happier moments.

Wisdom

Wisdom entails applying knowledge and experience with insight and good judgement. It grows through personal experiences and learning from others. Wisdom is linked to continuous learning and involves being brave and courageous. We all carry wisdom from our unique life journeys, and by embracing our own wisdom and being curious about others', we can foster growth and understanding. Sharing wisdom with empathy and compassion allows for ongoing learning and deeper connections. We must understand that we all carry wisdom, embrace the wisdom we hold, and be curious about the wisdom of others. Sharing wisdom through curiosity and empathy allows for ongoing learning with compassion for oneself and others.

Gathering Learning and Understanding: The Infinite Game

We easily get sidetracked from what truly matters when we focus on competing with others instead of staying authentic to ourselves. When we view others as worthy competitors who can help us grow and better understand our goals, it shifts competition from a win/lose mindset to a learning experience. This perspective values collaboration and the strength of working together to achieve greater outcomes. It highlights the balance between dependence (relying on others), independence (self-reliance), and interdependence (working together for mutual success), recognising that interdependence often leads to the most meaningful progress.

Confidence

Imagine if confidence weren't a barrier. What self-talk stops us from pursuing the things that truly matter? Let's explore how we perceive confidence in others, how it feels, and how we believe it should feel. Consider the pursuit of perfection and Brené Brown's insight that shame is often close behind when perfectionism is in control. Confidence is about discovering how to become our best selves and creating room to chase our dreams. Embracing new ventures with the enthusiasm and courage of a beginner can lead to significant growth. In the end, our only competition is ourselves as we strive to learn, grow, and clarify our goals and achievements.

Boundaries

Boundaries act like energy fields that protect our mind, body, and spirit. Recognising our triggers can allow us to reset and move forward, which supports our well-being when our boundaries are crossed. Brené Brown's concept of 'living BIG' encourages us to Be in our Integrity while being Generous in our assumptions about others. This means staying true to our values, holding firm to what's important to us, and assuming the best intentions from others. Combining strong boundaries with generosity and integrity can create healthier, more compassionate relationships with ourselves and others.

Change

As someone much wiser than me (my husband!) says, change is inevitable except from a vending machine!

Change is inevitable, and we must understand how we react to unforeseen, rapid, or planned change and sometimes even change we have strived for and integrated. Understanding what sustains and steadies us through change can enable us to embrace the future with a positive mindset.

Life is like a path we can move along with purpose and intention. Yet unexpected challenges can arise, requiring us to adapt. By discussing these turbulent times and how we navigate them, we empower ourselves to tap into our wisdom and keep moving forward.

The Wisdom in Anxiety

Anxiety, according to Tracy Dennis-Tiwary, is apprehension about our uncertain, imagined future and the vigilance that keeps us on high alert.

The wisdom of anxiety lies in its ability to alert us to potential threats and challenges, prompting us to take necessary action to address them. In moderation, anxiety can serve as a natural defence mechanism, helping us stay vigilant and focused in situations that require attention. It can motivate us to prepare for the future, make necessary changes, or seek support when needed.

Ultimately, the wisdom of anxiety lies in recognising it as a signal from our minds and bodies, urging us to pay attention to our surroundings and take appropriate steps to safeguard our mental and emotional health. To fully embrace this wisdom, we must also consider the positive outcome. Stepping up to jump off a diving board could be anxiety provoking, but the possibility of an exhilarating dive draws us to the diving board. The physical reaction to anxiety is also the same as excitement, so when you are at those diving board moments, do you tell yourself that you are anxious or excited? Which would serve you better?

Reflection

You are either in your bed or in your shoes, so it pays to invest in both.
—John Wildsmith

On reflection, it's fascinating how something as ordinary as shoes can carry such rich stories and meanings. Exploring the narratives behind people's footwear offers a creative way to delve into our personal values and stories. My experiences at UCD, where walking on different surfaces evoked unique feelings and memories, highlight the profound connection between our shoes and how we navigate life. The simple act of walking can reflect our inner selves and our relationship with the world around us.

The notion that identical shoe pairs purchased over time can illustrate subtle changes and growth is quite moving, reminding us of our continuous, often unnoticed evolution. An amusing anecdote about an old girlfriend's comment that shoes reveal much about a person, followed by a breakup, adds humour and irony, showing how symbols like shoes can hold significant meaning in relationships, even if we're unaware.

This book aims to foster meaningful connections and conversations, encouraging people to share parts of themselves through their footwear choices. It demonstrates how storytelling can reveal insights and understanding from unexpected sources. Shoes as a tool for self-exploration are accessible and fun, inviting reflection on personal narratives and values through the lens of everyday items.

The diverse stories shared through photos and anecdotes vividly illustrate the multifaceted role shoes play, from giving joy to helping people navigate challenges, from marking milestones to providing moments of humour or vulnerability. Each pair tells a unique story that mirrors the wearer's experiences and aspirations.

Self-reflective questions offer a structured yet flexible way to assess our relationship with shoes and ourselves, revealing our preferences, our values, and the environments we navigate. I aim to promote self-awareness and understanding by sharing shoe stories that allow us to find common ground, celebrate differences, and appreciate our diverse journeys.

This book empowers us to live more intentionally, aligning choices with values and aspirations, reminding us that even mundane objects can lead to self-discovery and growth. Exploring our world through shoes becomes a fun segue into meaningful conversations.

My coaching approach provides a self-assessment tool to navigate personal and key relationships. By engaging in meaningful conversations and uncovering insights, we aim to enrich personal and relational understanding.

Using shoes as a metaphor, I offer a tangible entry point for reflecting on aspects of life like habits, listening skills, values, and purpose. Each session focuses on a specific area, offering exercises that encourage self-awareness and growth. For instance, 'Habits Every Day – Embracing Choice' explores alignment with values, while 'Listening Skills' delves into communication.

By anchoring discussions in everyday experiences and using relatable metaphors like shoes, I make the process engaging and accessible, helping to connect people with the material and apply it in life. This book offers a holistic approach to personal development, focusing on self-awareness, communication, and growth. It encourages gratitude for being unique and resourceful and embracing each day as an opportunity for transformation.

> *I wake up in the morning, just glad my boots are on.*
> —Bruce Springsteen, "Western Stars"

This shoe story is coming to a close for now. I hope this book has been an enjoyable read for you, that it has created a thinking space that can be amalgamated into your day.

I would like to leave you in a place of knowing and valuing your own uniqueness. There is no one the same as you anywhere. Your voice and ideas are worthy. Find the spaces where you have a sense of belonging, where your footsteps bring joy as they arrive. This is where you thrive, but there is also much to learn and grow in by stepping into challenge, the places where your heart quickens with excitement about the possibilities ahead. We learn how to do difficult things by doing difficult things.

Work With Lucy

Take the road less travelled, but first get new shoes.
—Anon

As a WACN (World Association of Coaching with Neuroscience)-registered coach with a strong foundation in neuroscience, I offer tailored sessions that prioritise building meaningful connections and encouraging personal growth. My aim is to assist you in confronting life's challenges with clarity and confidence by identifying and capitalising on your unique strengths.

Whether you're looking to improve personal relationships or explore new ventures, I provide the insights and support needed to progress. Together we'll discover new ways of thinking and acting that foster a happier, more fulfilling life. I strive to empower you to access your inner wisdom, transcend self-imposed limitations, and create narratives that present new opportunities and choices. We'll explore whether your personal stories are limiting your potential or can be transformed into powerful insights for your future.

Join me on this journey of self-discovery, where your creativity unlocks endless possibilities. Initiate your journey with a free, no-obligation discovery call by mailing or by contacting me directly via my website and see how I can assist you in realising your full potential.

If you would like to work with me, I would invite you to reach out to me at lucy.cronly@gmail.com or check out the different services offered at https://lucycronlycoaching.ie.

Bonus Items

1. Download your complimentary workbook

Avail of the complimentary workbook containing questions and prompts covered in this book by emailing Lucy on lucy.cronly@gmail.com.

2. A History of Shoes and Fun Facts

The history of different shoes across cultures reveals fascinating stories of adaptation, craftsmanship, and societal change. From clogs in Holland to ballet slippers, each type of shoe was designed to meet the unique demands of environment, culture, and available resources. Let's explore some of these, starting with specific examples and working through their evolution.

Dutch clogs, or klompen, are iconic wooden shoes that have been worn in Holland for centuries. Originally, clogs were designed to protect feet from the wet, marshy Dutch terrain. Made from local woods like poplar or willow, they provided a sturdy, waterproof shield against muddy fields and rough surfaces. Over time, they became a symbol of Dutch rural life. As industrialisation brought cobbled streets, clogs evolved to include leather tops and wooden soles for better navigating urban environments. Today, they're still worn by some farmers but are also cherished as cultural symbols, often intricately decorated.

The Japanese geta, a type of wooden sandal, was designed to suit the often rainy and muddy conditions of ancient Japan. The raised platform helped keep feet dry, elevated above dirt and water. Traditionally made from wood, they were tied to the feet with cloth straps. Geta were originally worn with a kimono or yukata (summer robe) but have since become part of modern fashion as well, often with a focus on tradition. Their distinctive clacking sound is often associated with summer festivals. Over time, geta have evolved to accommodate urban life, often featuring rubber bottoms for better traction on pavement.

Moccasins, made from soft leather, were a practical and versatile shoe used by Indigenous peoples of North America. They were crafted to suit the specific terrain, from the plains to forested regions. Flexible and lightweight, they allowed wearers to move silently through the woods – a crucial advantage in hunting and combat. Materials like deer or buffalo hide were readily available, and the shoes often featured intricate beadwork or quillwork reflecting cultural significance. As European colonisation altered Indigenous lifeways, moccasins became a blend of traditional and modern styles, with some adaptations for harder, paved surfaces in cities.

Ballet shoes evolved in Europe during the seventeenth century, designed to allow dancers maximum movement and grace. The soft slipper, later evolving into the pointe shoe, gave dancers the ability to dance en pointe, balancing on the tips of their toes. Pointe shoes, introduced in the early nineteenth century, were originally made from leather and later evolved into more flexible satin shoes with reinforced tips. These shoes are highly specialised, constructed with layers of material to support the dancer's foot in an unnatural position. The delicate design reflects the need for both flexibility and strength, matching the artistic demands of ballet's evolution.

Irish dance shoes are divided into two main types: soft shoes (ghillies) and hard shoes. Soft shoes, made of black leather with criss crossed laces, are similar to ballet shoes and are used for lighter, more fluid movements in Irish dancing. Hard shoes, on the other hand, are akin to tap shoes, producing the distinctive rhythmic sound that Irish dance is famous for. These hard shoes developed from the Irish tradition of dancing on wooden floors, where the tapping created its own percussive accompaniment to the music. As Irish dance evolved from a local tradition to an international phenomenon (popularised in the 1990s by shows like *Riverdance*), the shoes adapted as well, incorporating new materials to enhance both sound and durability on modern stages.

Crocs, a brand of foam clogs, were first introduced in 2002 as boating shoes, known for their comfort, water resistance, and durability. Made from a lightweight, proprietary material called Croslite, Crocs quickly gained popularity among boaters, health care workers, and other professionals who needed functional, comfortable footwear.

By 2007, the brand had exploded into the mainstream, with millions of pairs sold worldwide. However, overexpansion and the 2008 recession led to financial struggles, forcing Crocs to downsize and refocus on its core clog product.

A resurgence came in the mid-2010s as the 'ugly fashion' trend redefined Crocs as a quirky, ironic style choice. High-profile collaborations with designers and celebrities, along with a rise in demand for comfort wear during the COVID-19 pandemic, helped Crocs make a strong comeback. Today, Crocs is a billion-dollar global brand, known for its unique, divisive aesthetic, comfort, and customization options like Jibbitz charms.

The development of shoes also tells a story about societal changes. Early shoes were often crafted from what was locally available – wood in forested regions, leather in areas with abundant wildlife, straw or cloth where plants were plentiful. As societies became more industrialised, footwear adapted to new materials and environments. For example, as people began to walk on cobblestones and later concrete, shoe soles became more durable, often with rubber or leather soles for longevity and comfort. Shoes like moccasins, originally crafted for soft forest floors, gained hard soles to suit the needs of urban living.

The rise of global trade also played a huge role. Leather, once a luxury material, became more widely available. Styles like the pointed shoes of the medieval era reflected the growing influence of fashion rather than pure function. In contrast, shoes like clogs, which were made for practicality, remained tied to the working class for much longer.

Footwear from different cultures, whether designed for protection, performance, or status, reflects the environments, materials, and social structures that shaped them. From the marshy fields of Holland to the graceful stages of ballet, shoes are a testament to how humans have adapted to the challenges of their world. And as society changed –bringing new materials, urbanisation, and fashion – shoes continued to evolve alongside it, transforming from simple necessities into complex cultural symbols.

Please Review

Dear Reader,

I would deeply appreciate it if you would spread the word about this publication. As a first-time author, I know your support can make a significant difference.

By telling others about this book, sharing about it on social media, or leaving a review online, you can help spread awareness, encourage open conversations, and foster personal growth among readers of all ages.

Thank you for being a part of this journey and helping to share the message of self-discovery and building meaningful connections and relationships that this book embodies.

—Lucy

Appendix 1

Dear [Recipient's Name],

I hope this message finds you well. I am currently working on an exciting book project centred around shoes and their profound impact on our lives. This book aims to explore how we move through life with intention, the choices we make in our footwear, and how these choices create moments of reflection and consideration, empower us, provide support, and help us become the best versions of ourselves.

I believe your insights and wisdom would greatly enrich the narrative of this book. I have prepared a short questionnaire to make things as easy as possible.

If you have any questions or would like to discuss this further, I am available for a chat over Zoom, phone or email at your convenience. Please feel free to reach out anytime.

Before any of your contributions are included in the book, I will send you a draft to review and will seek your approval.

Here are some of the questions I would love to hear your thoughts on:

1. Look down at your feet. What story do your shoes tell today?
2. What do you think about using shoes as a segue into meaningful conversations?

3. Do you know someone who could buy you shoes that you love without discussing them with you? Who would this be and why?
4. Have you ever admired someone's shoes and been surprised by the story behind the shoes? Can you share the story?
5. What is your show plan for today or tomorrow, and why?

Additionally, if you have a personal shoe story you would like to share, I would be thrilled to include it in the book.

Thank you for considering this request. I look forward to hearing from you and potentially sharing your unique perspective with readers around the world.

Kind regards,

Lucy

References

Standing on the shoulders of giants

I would like to acknowledge some of the very smart thinking authors, poets, artists that inspired me along the way:

Brene Brown

There is great wisdom in Brene's work and many wonderful books. Her book Atlas of the Heart resonated with my thinking writing this book and her work on Wholehearted living

Brene Brown Atlas of the Heart, Mapping meaningful connection and the language of human experience. 2021 Ebury Publishing.

Simon Sinek

Simon Sinek's work is so accessible and created thinking not just doing for me. Knowing my purpose has enabled me to do difficult things because I am clear about my goal.

Simon Sinek Find your Why 2019 Penguin Random House UK
Simon Sinek The Infinite Game 2019 Penguin LLC

Tracy Dennis

Tracy's work is inspirational around managing anxiety and the wisdom that lies in our anxiety. Harnessing it and putting it to use to create balance and keep us safe is invaluable.

Tracy Dennis Tiwary Future Tense. Why anxiety is good for you (even though it feels bad) 2022 Harper Press

The quotes throughout are used as they resonated so well with the story. Each author had a vision of how we move around in the world and I hope by sharing their work you might tap into their wisdom a little further, there are nuggets of wonderful wisdom to be had.

Morgan Harper Nichols has an amazing Instagram page with many beautiful artworks and quotations.

Dr Seuss is from the book 'Oh The Places you will Go' 2017 Harper Collins Publishers

Donna Ashworth has a website of beautiful quotes and books at www.donnaashworth.com

Linda Hogan, Dwellings: A Spiritual History of the Living World

Mary Oliver This Wild and precious life 2024 Random House Inc

Pat Schneider The Weight of love Negative Capability Press 2019

Bruce Springsteen, Western Stars, Album Western Stars 2019